Faerie Houses

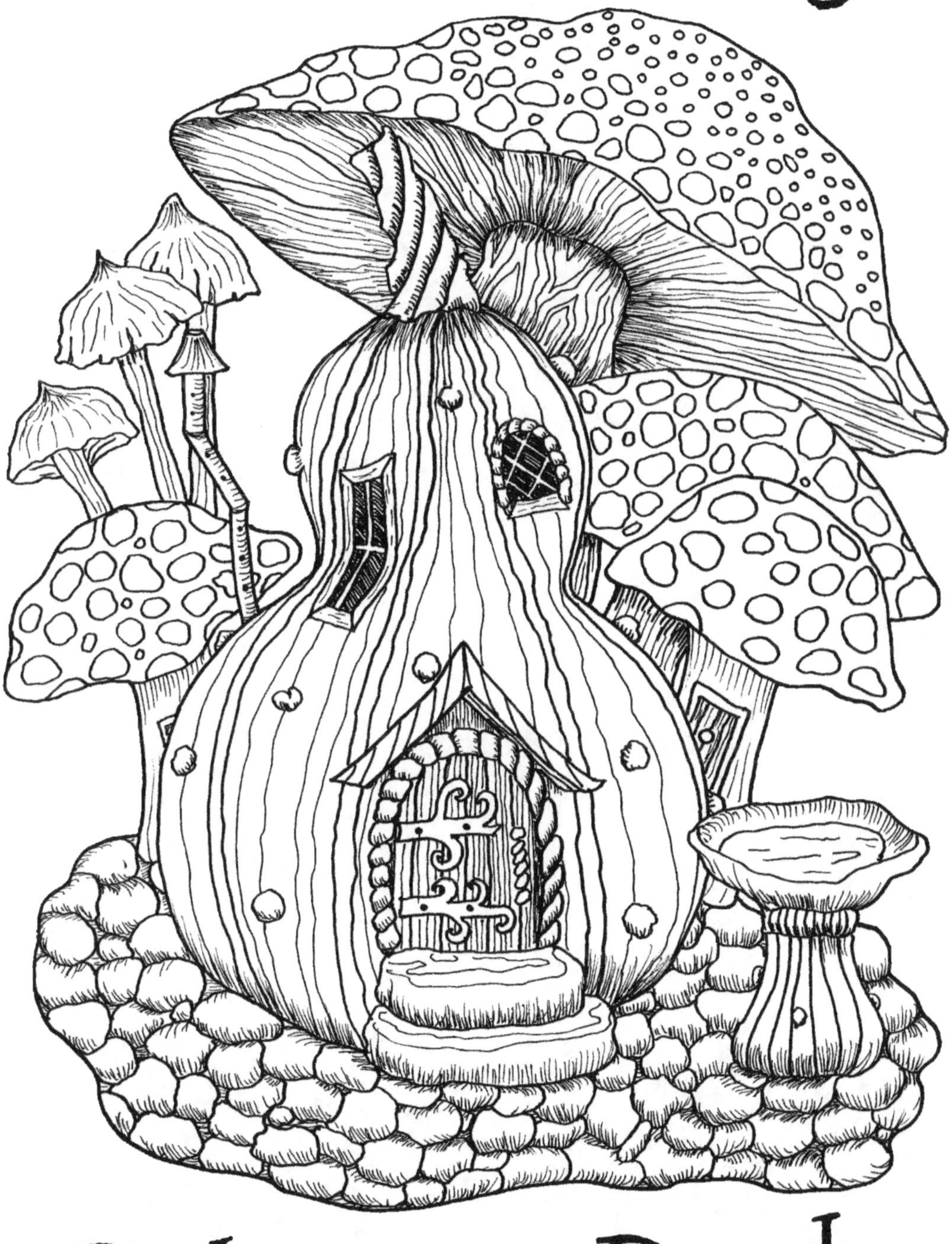

Coloring Book

Stephany Elsworth

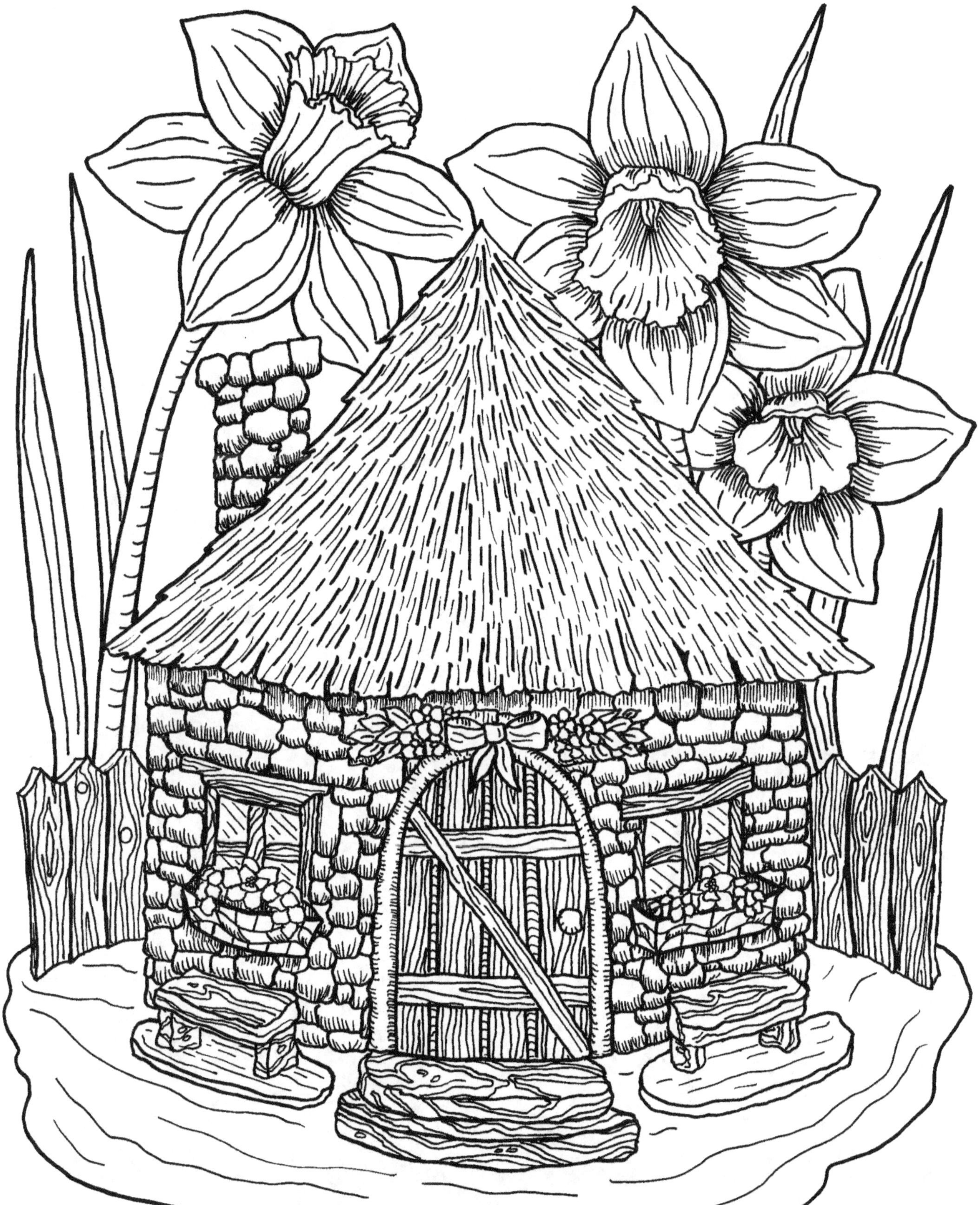

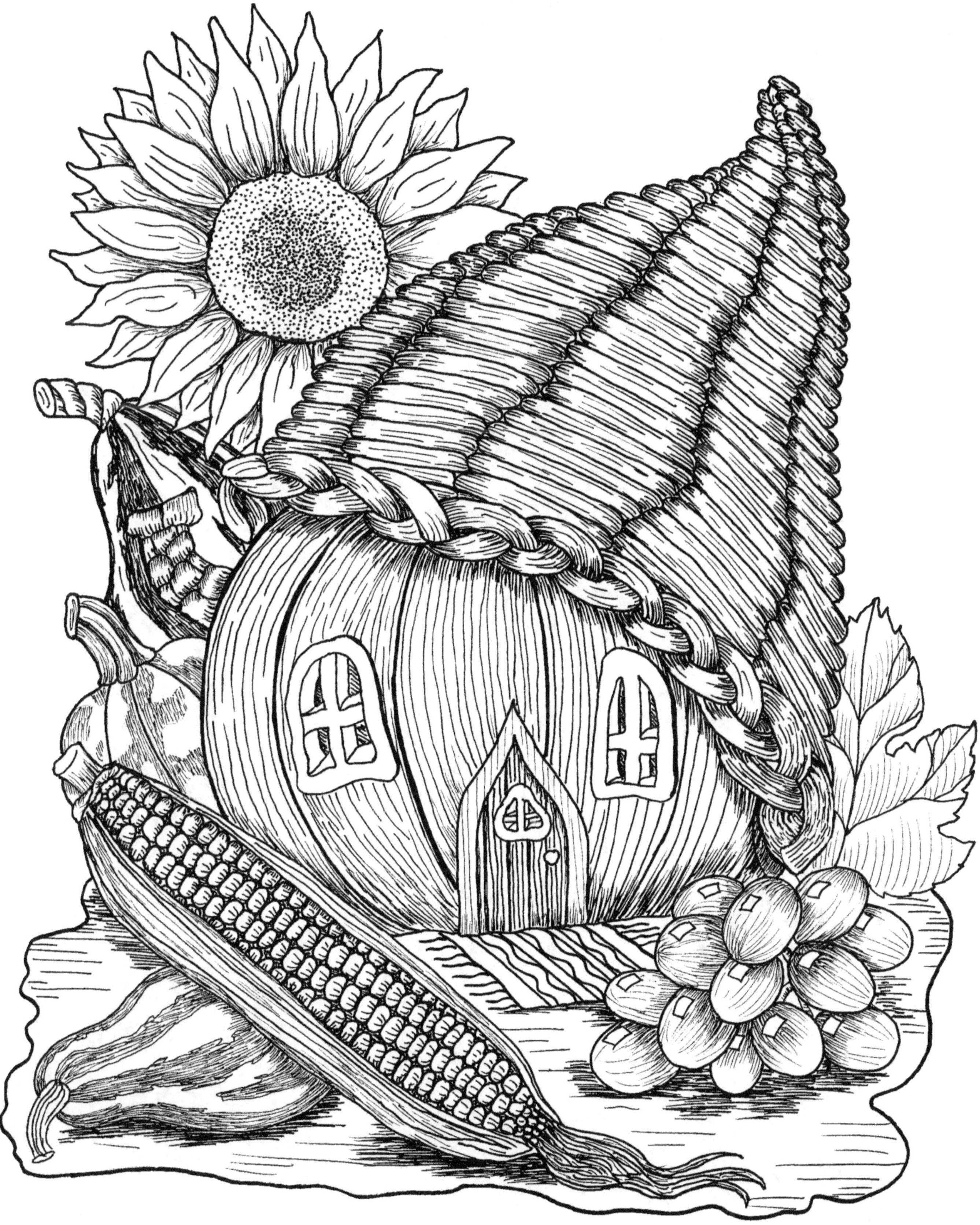

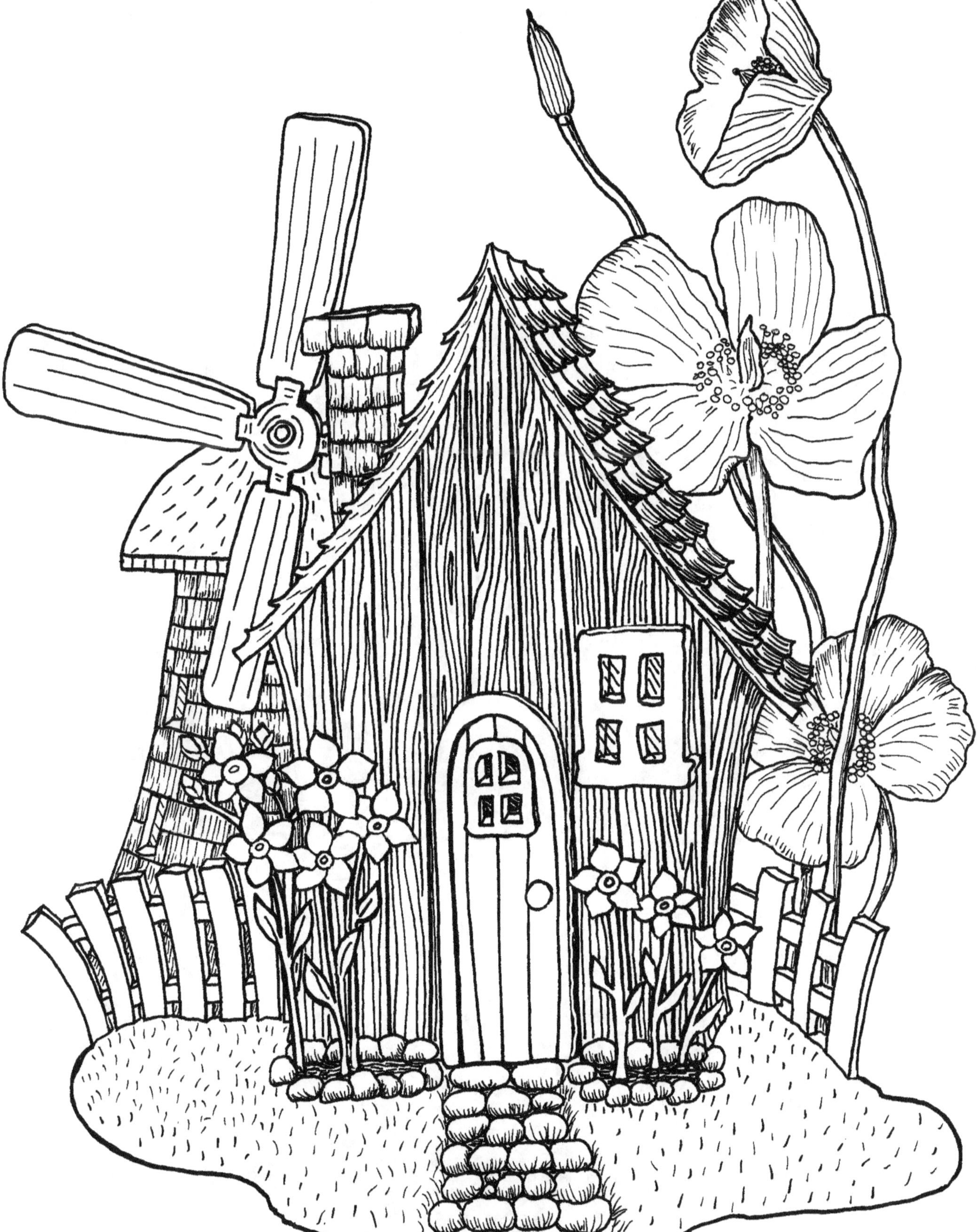

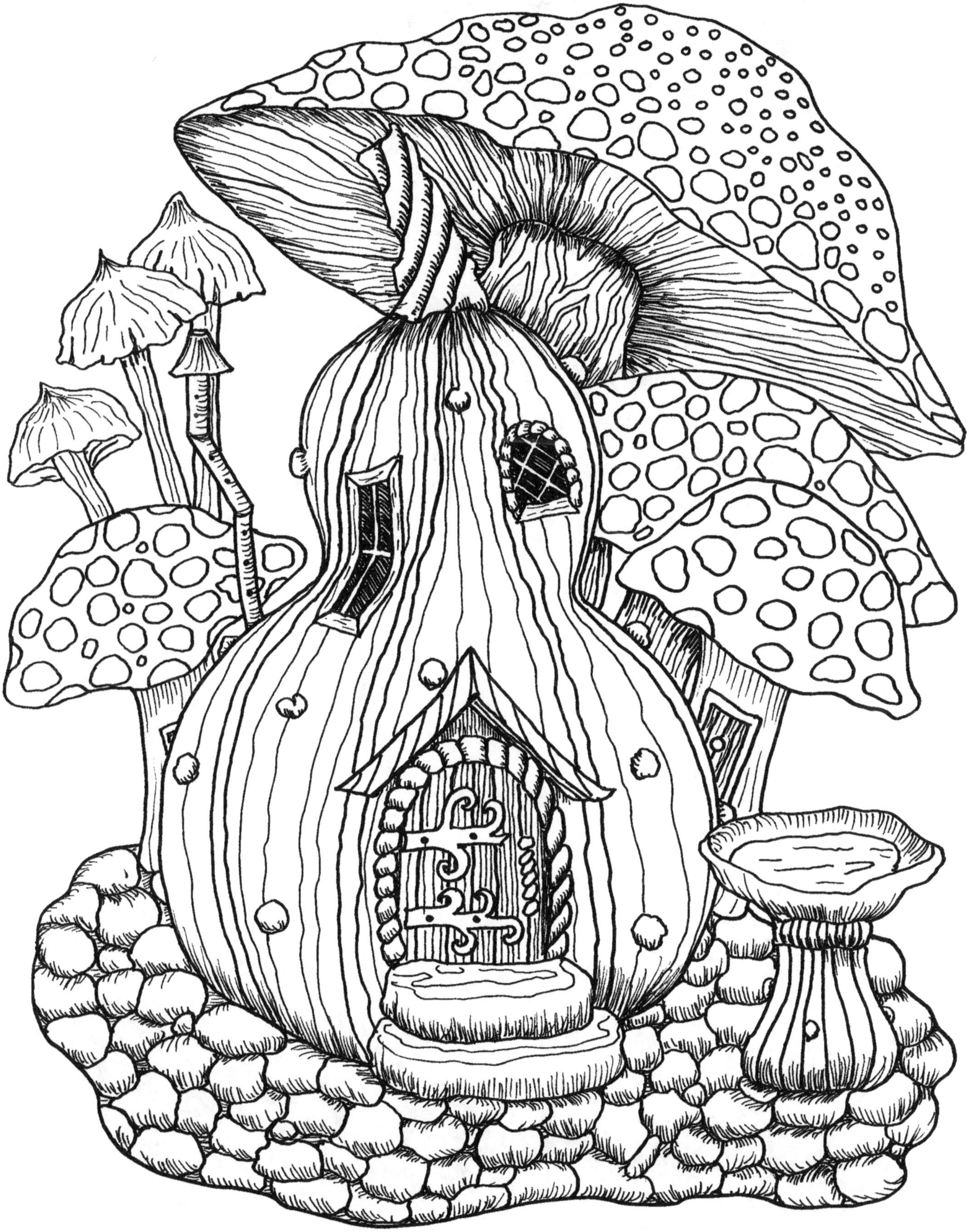

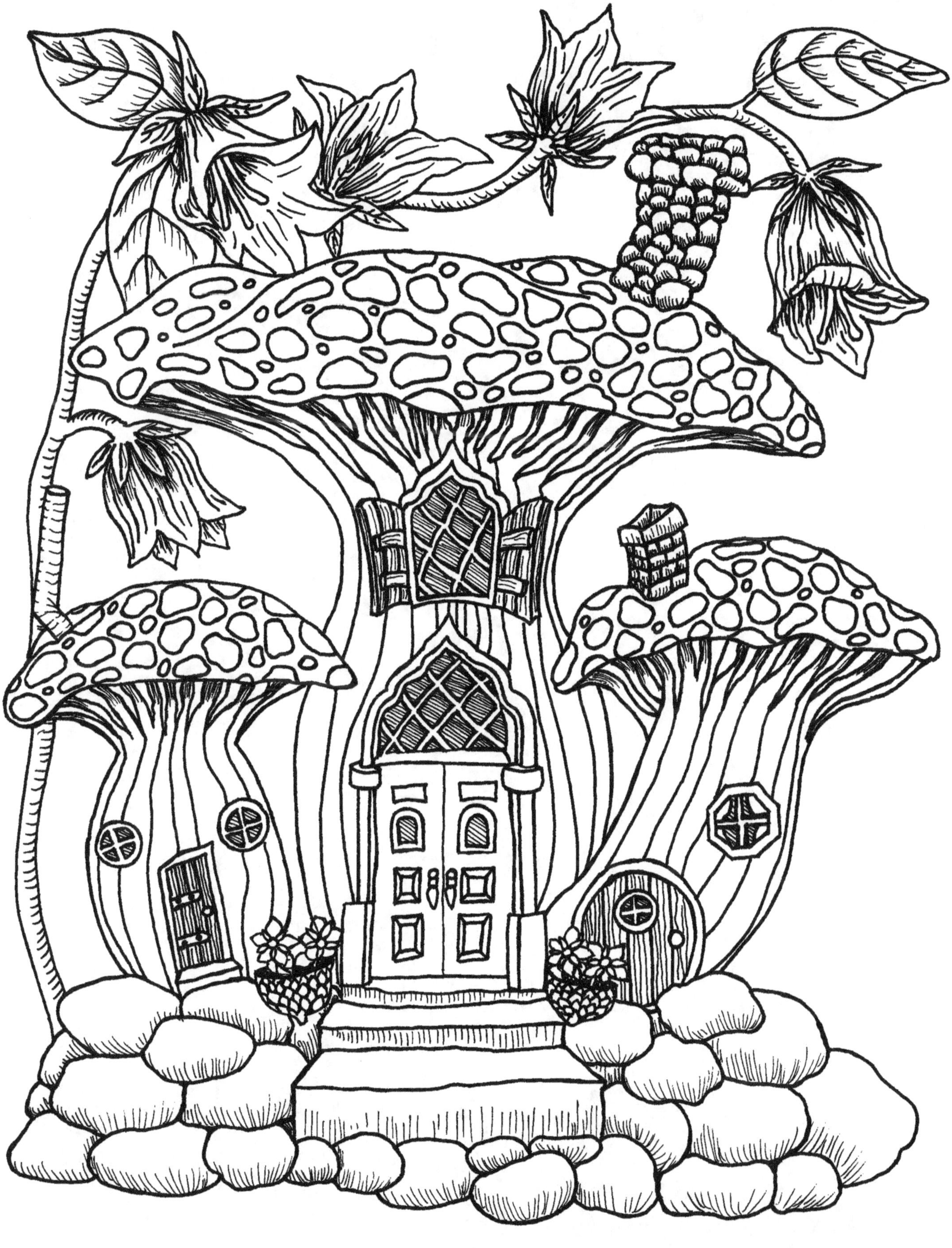

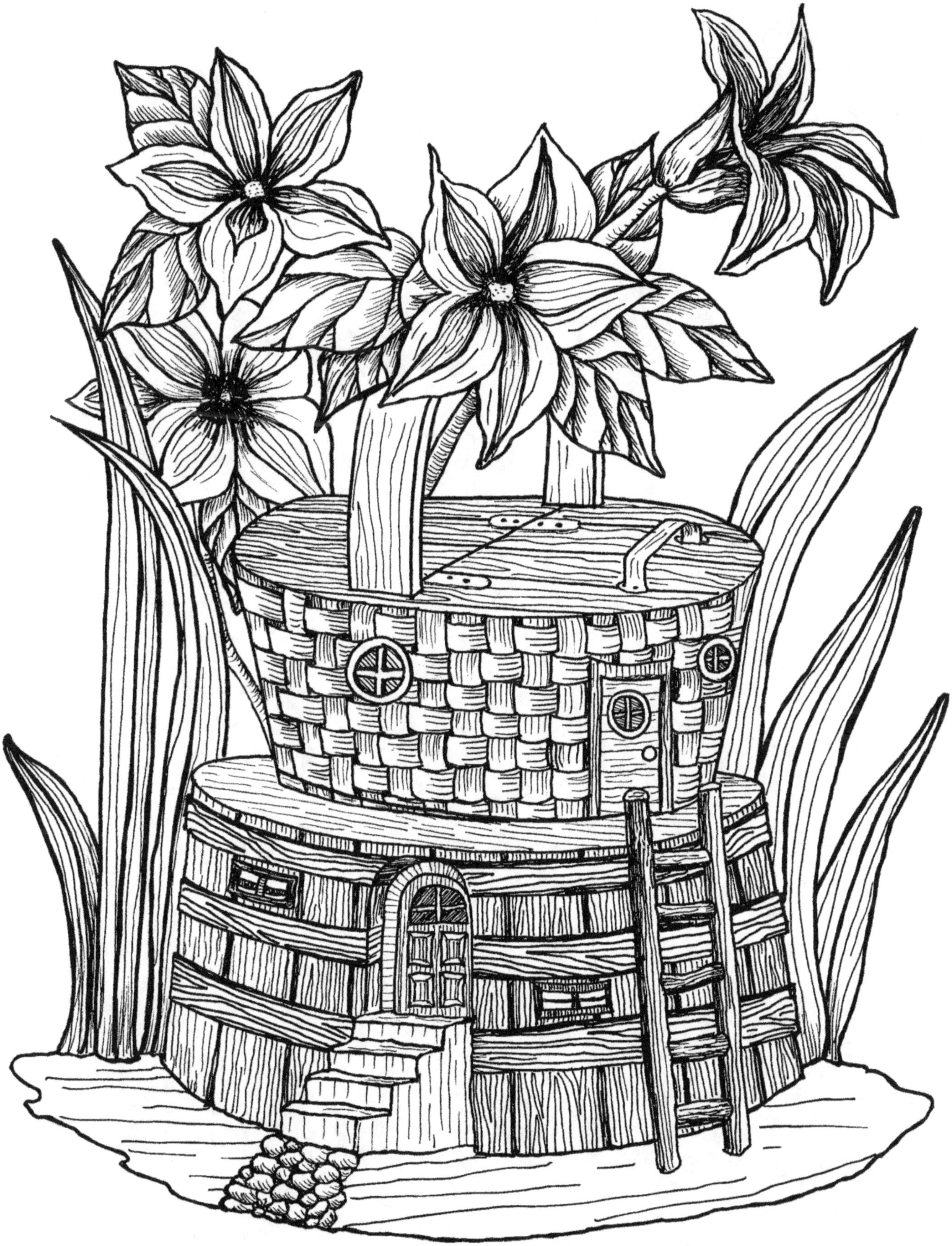

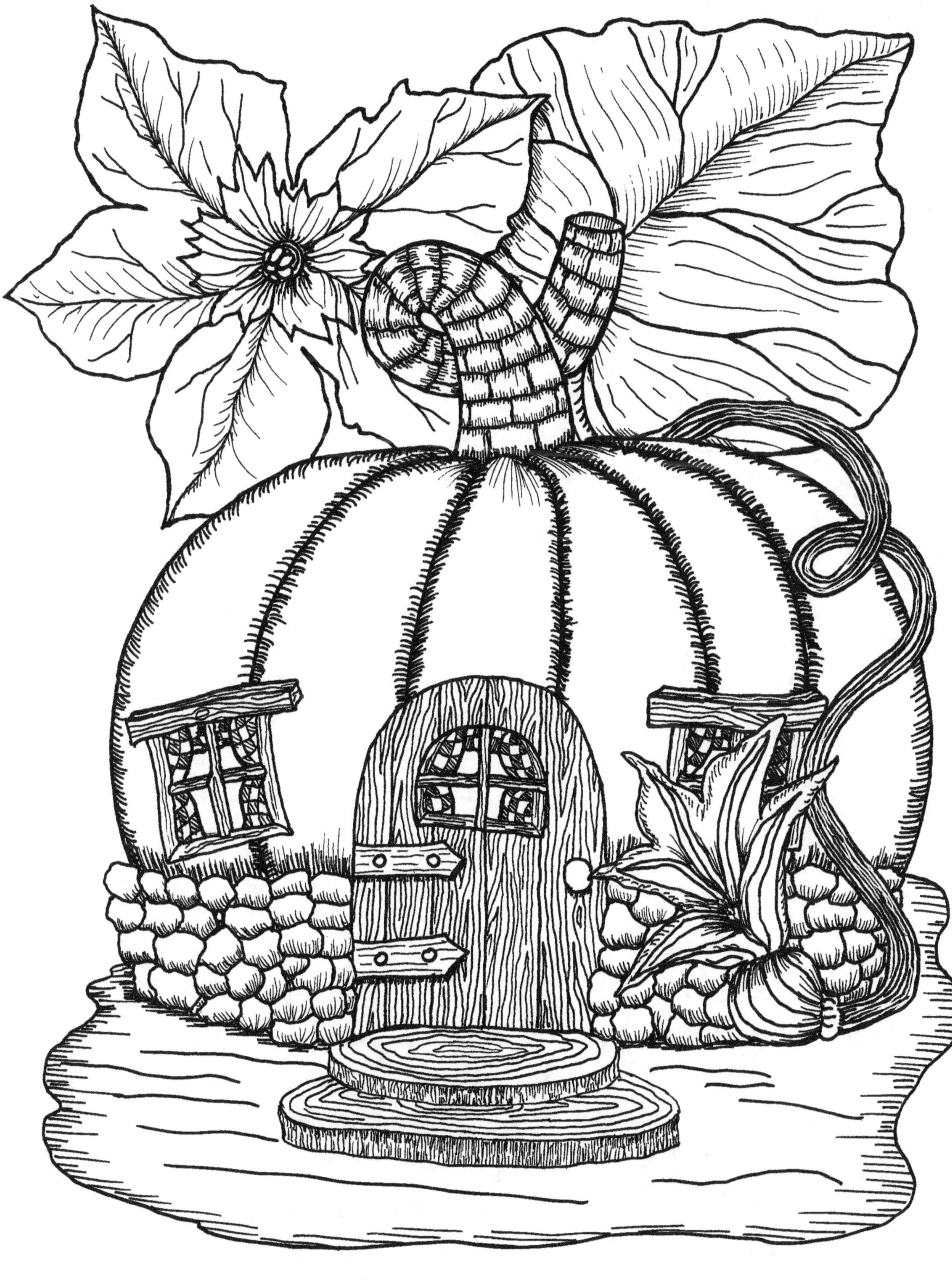

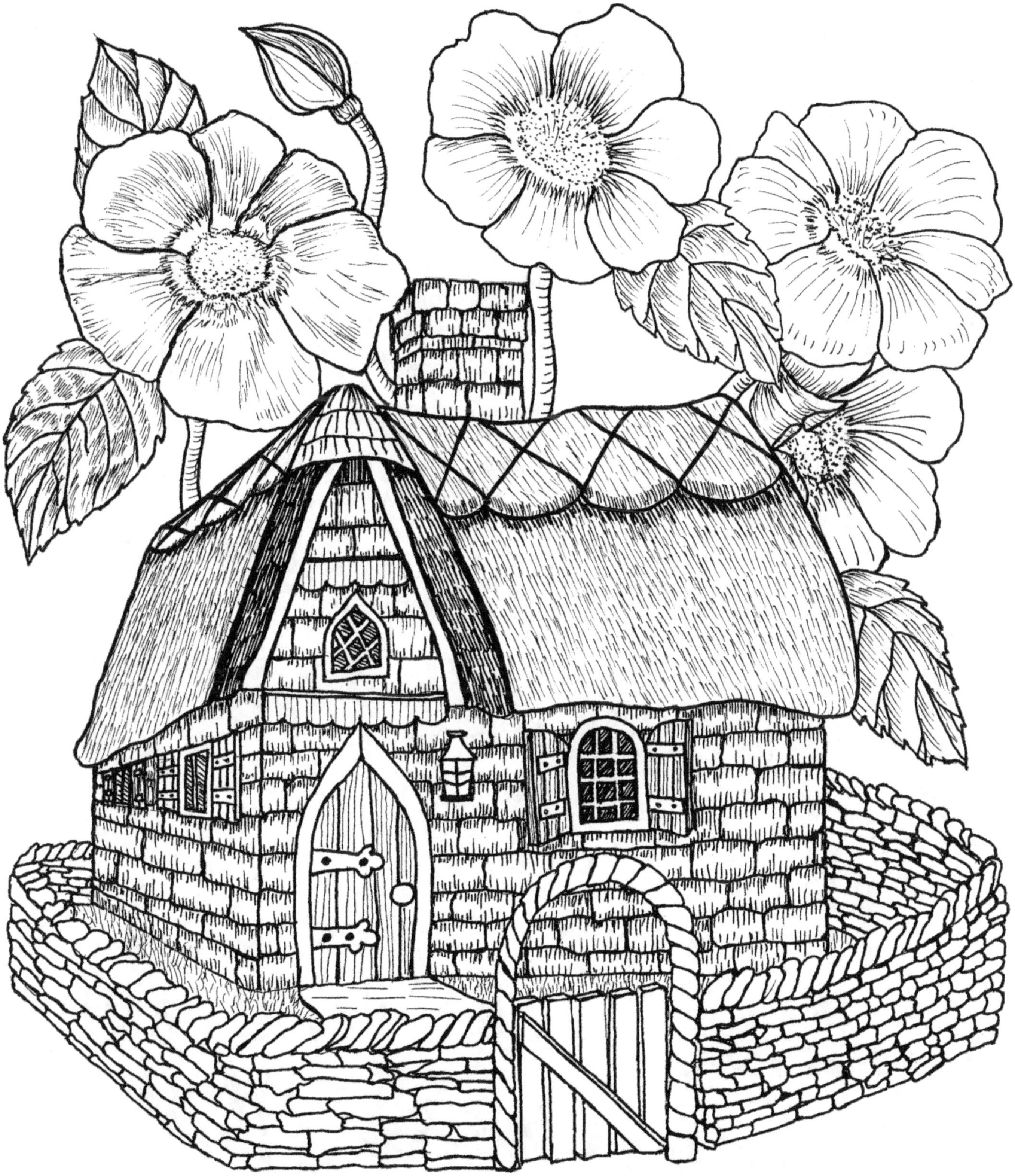

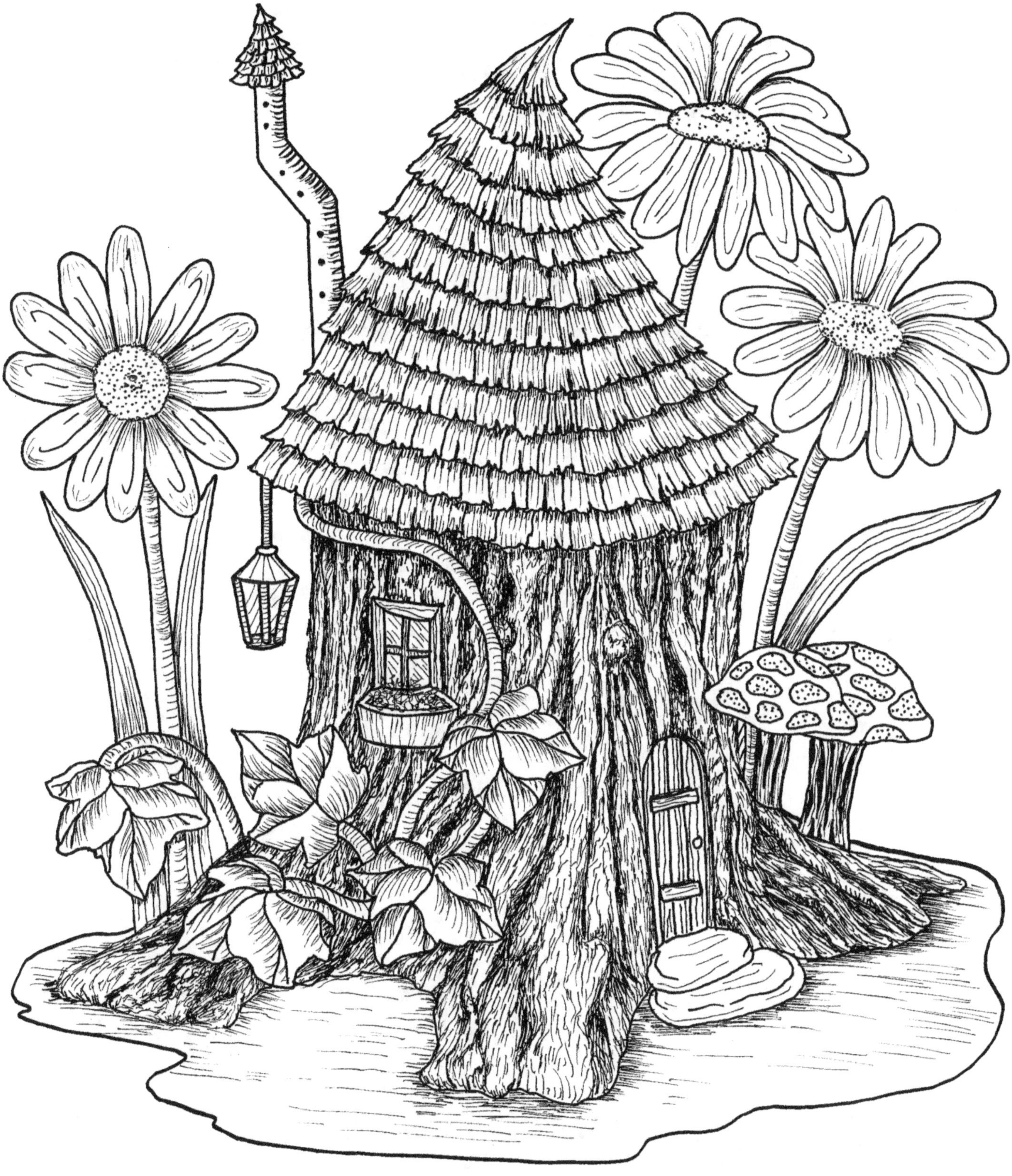

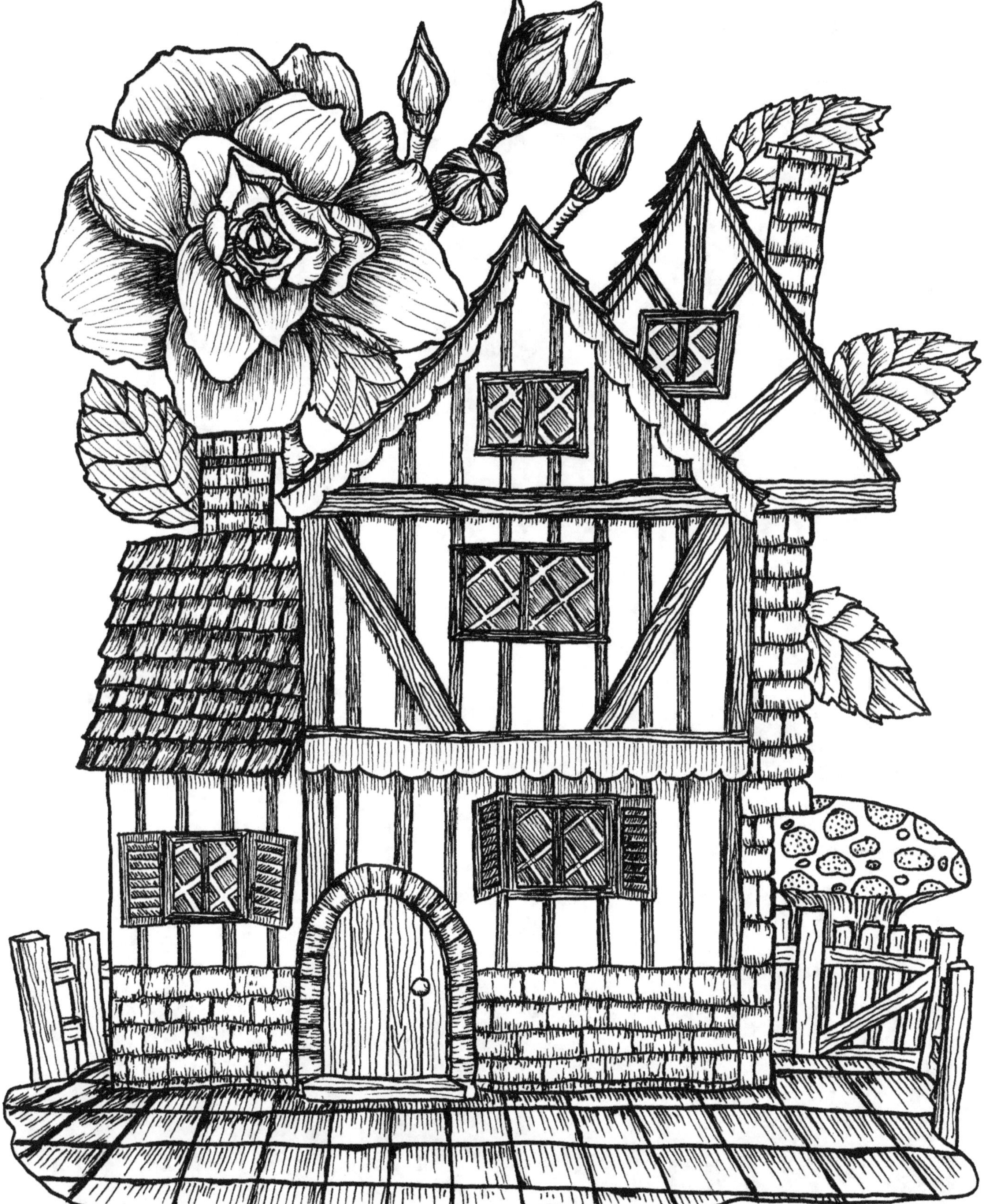

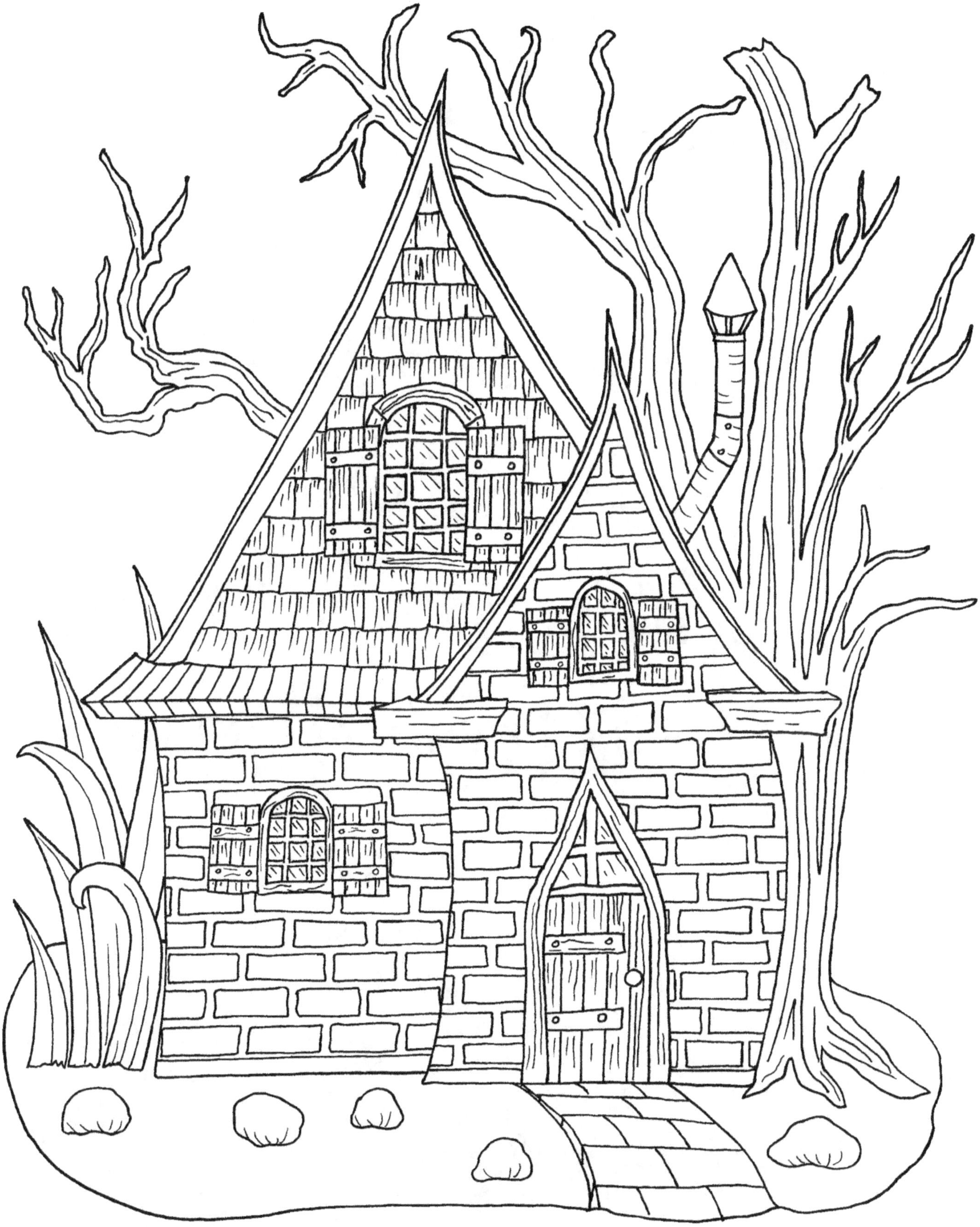

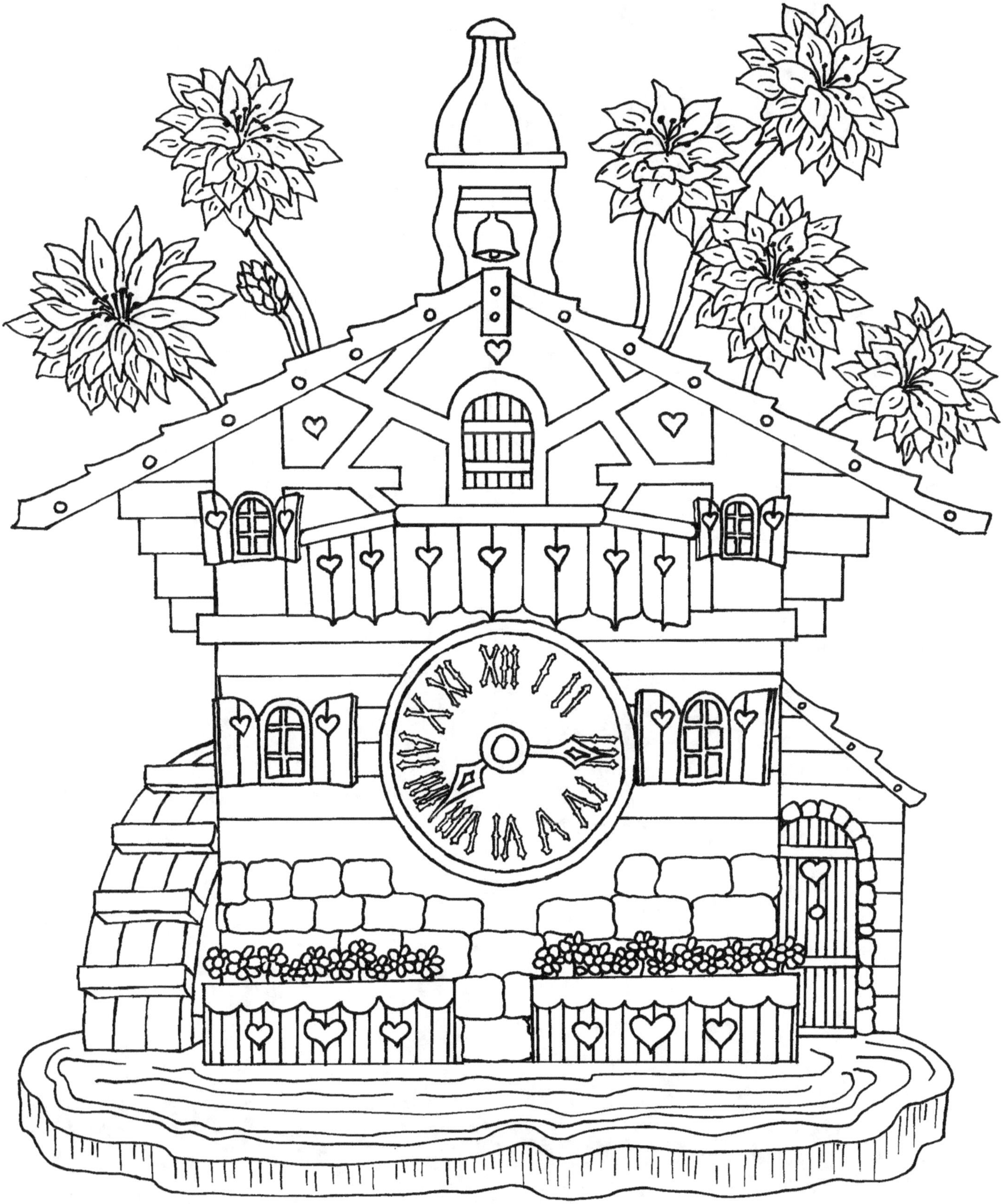

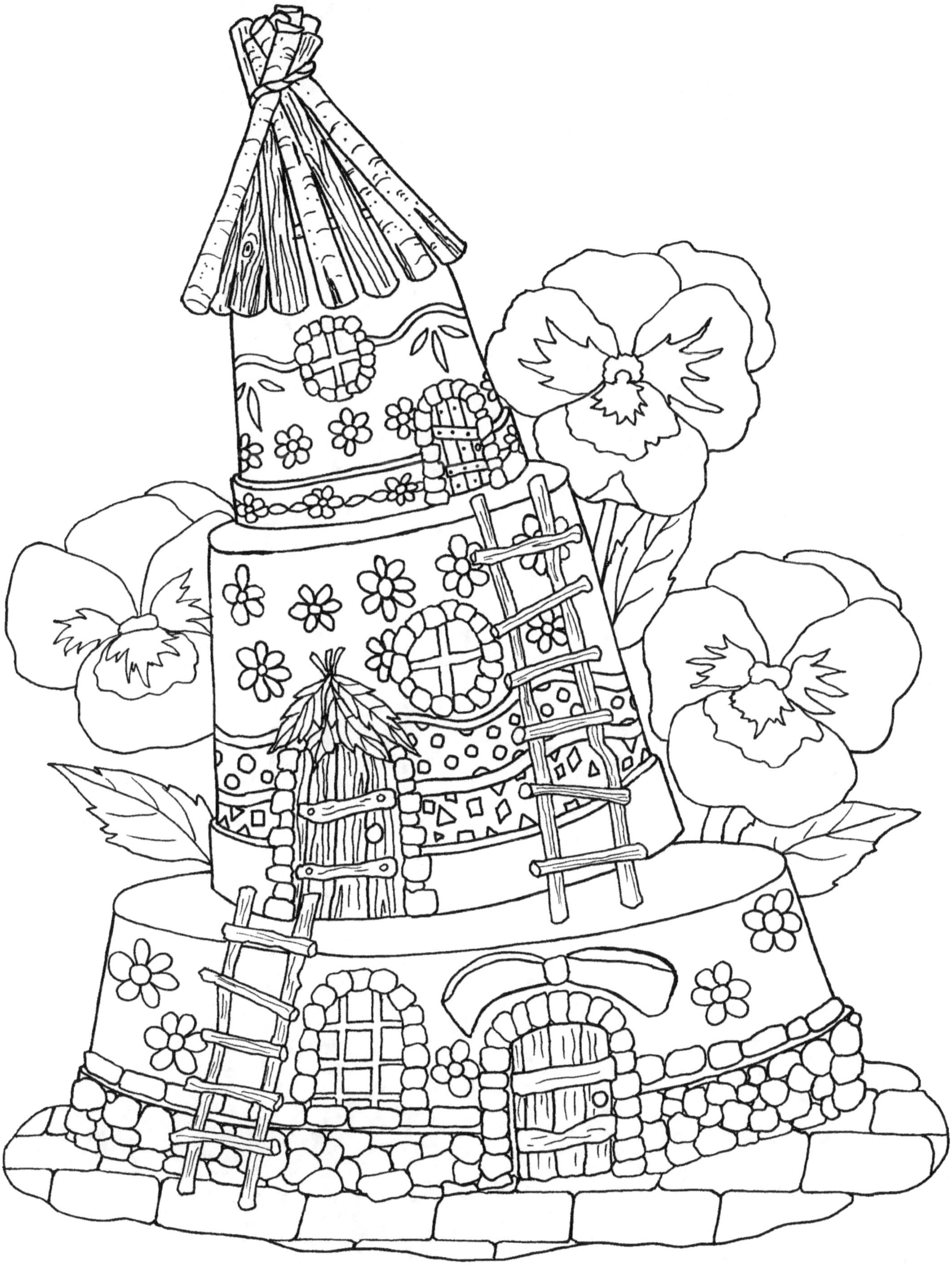

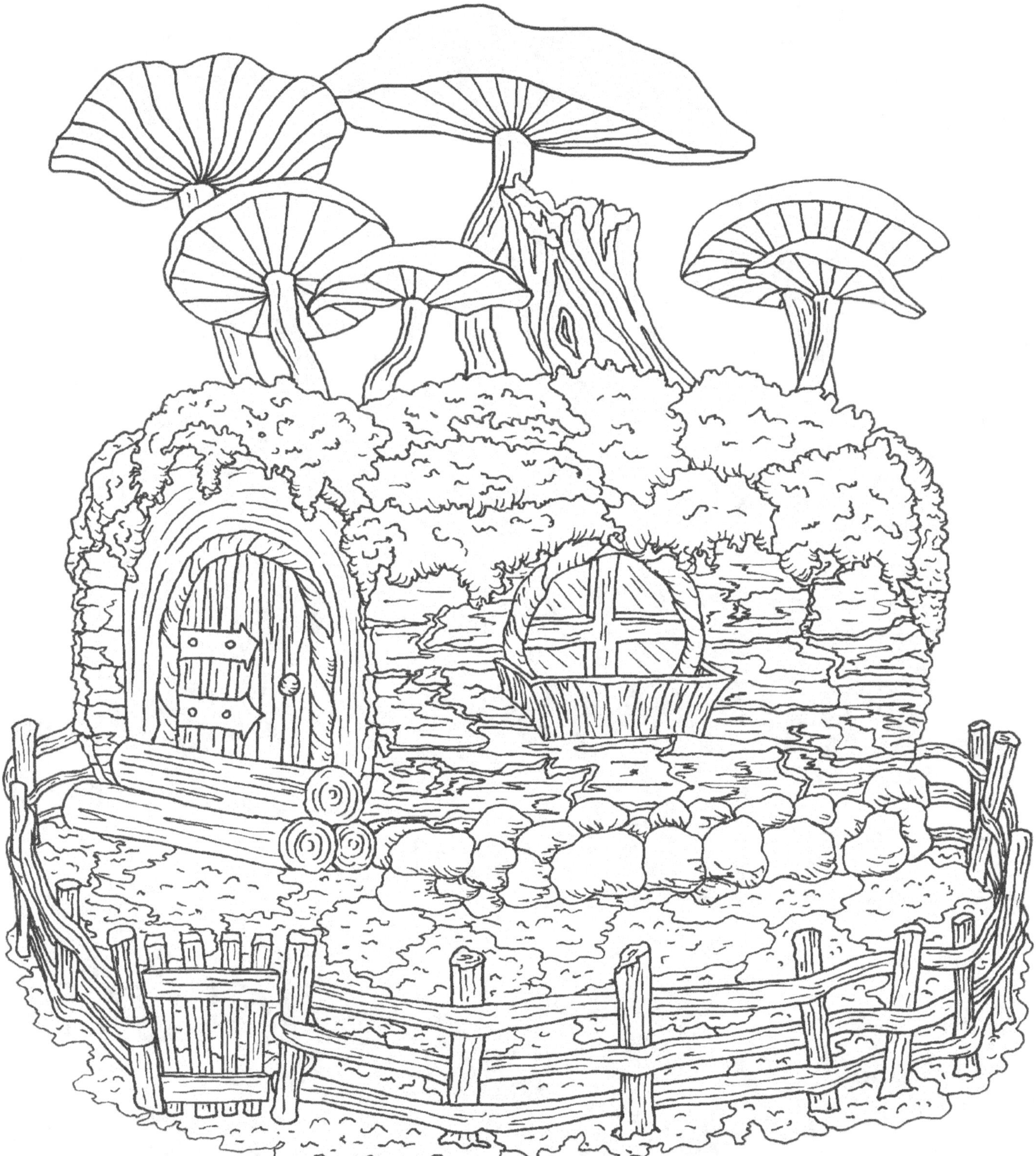

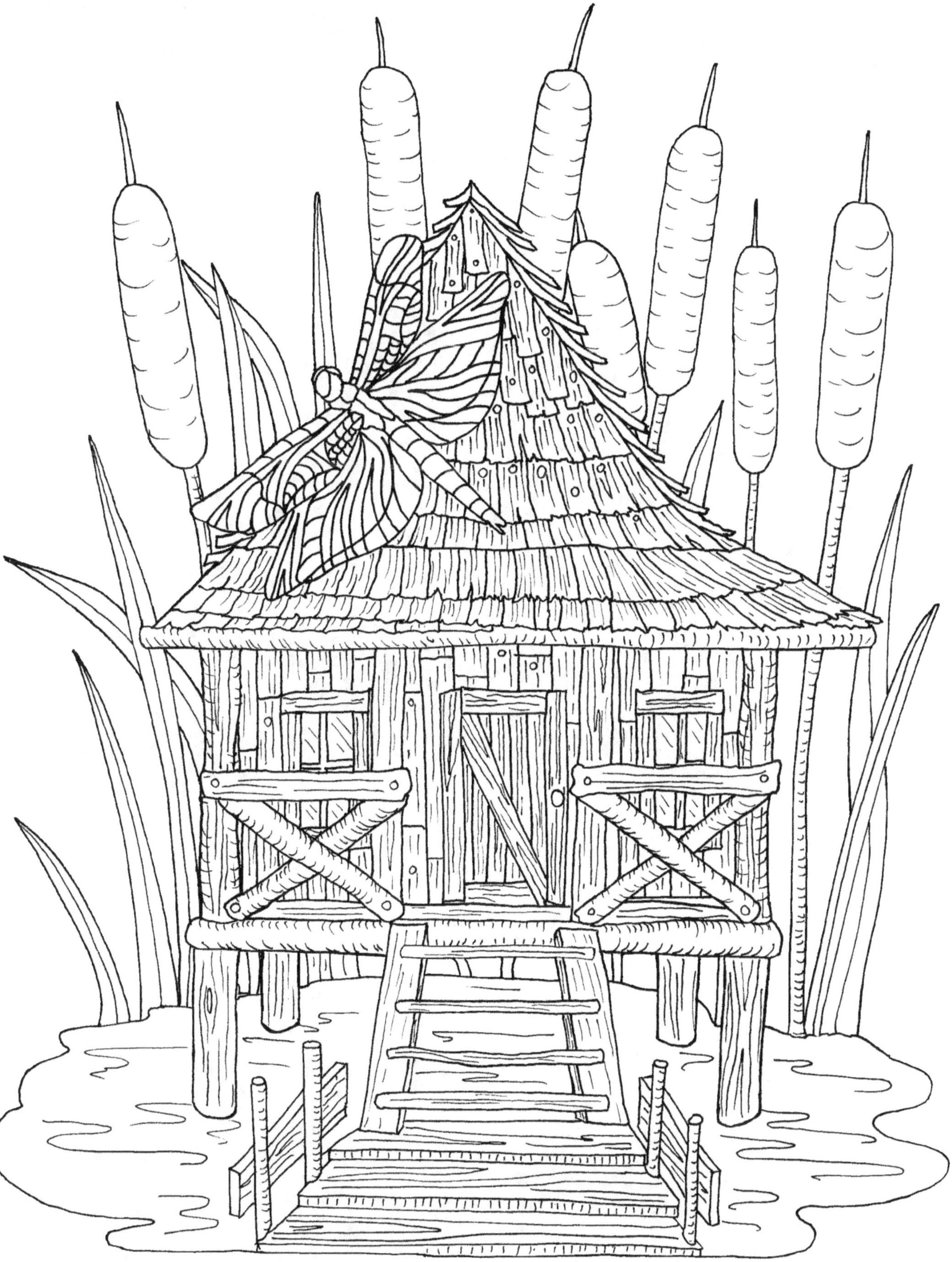

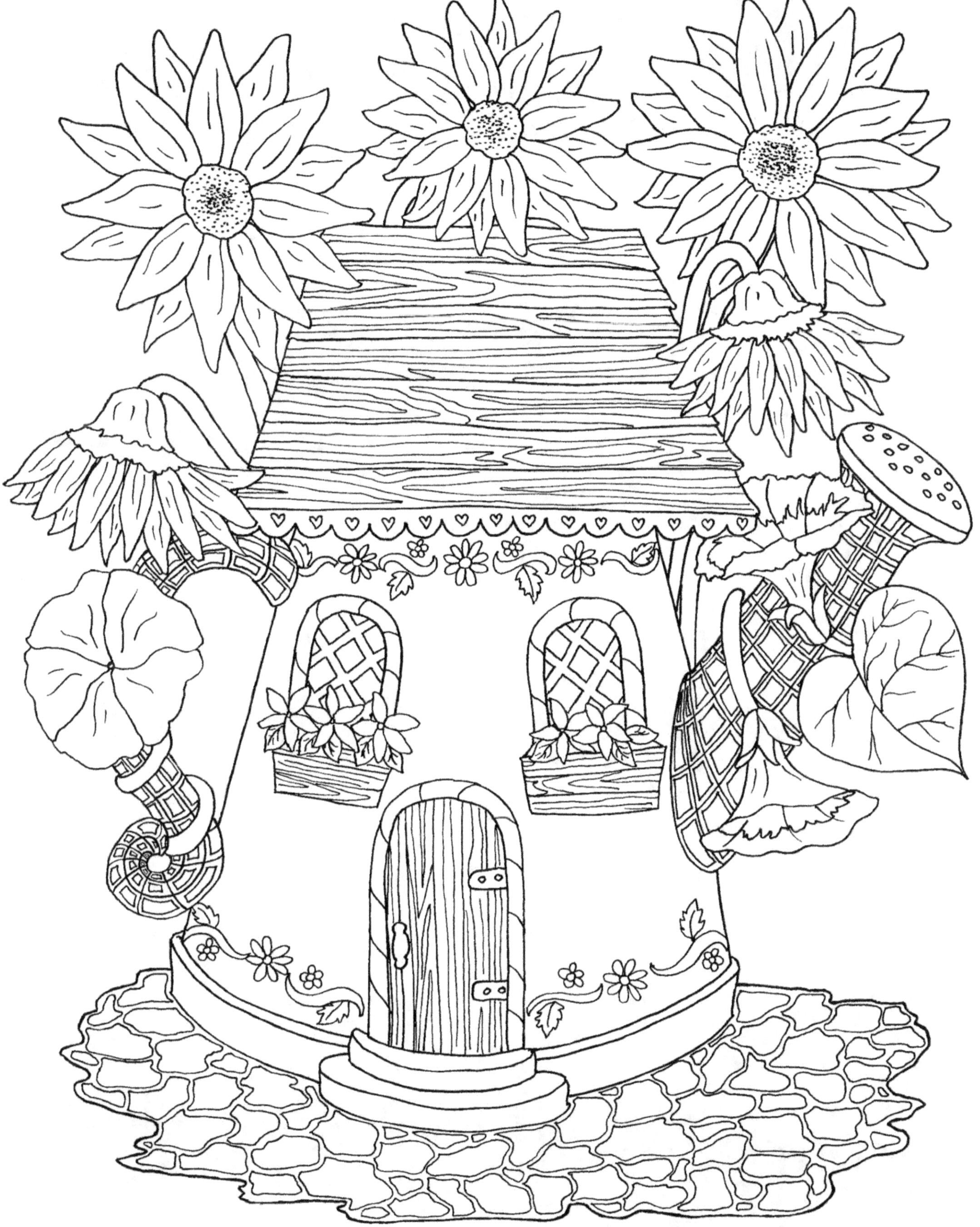

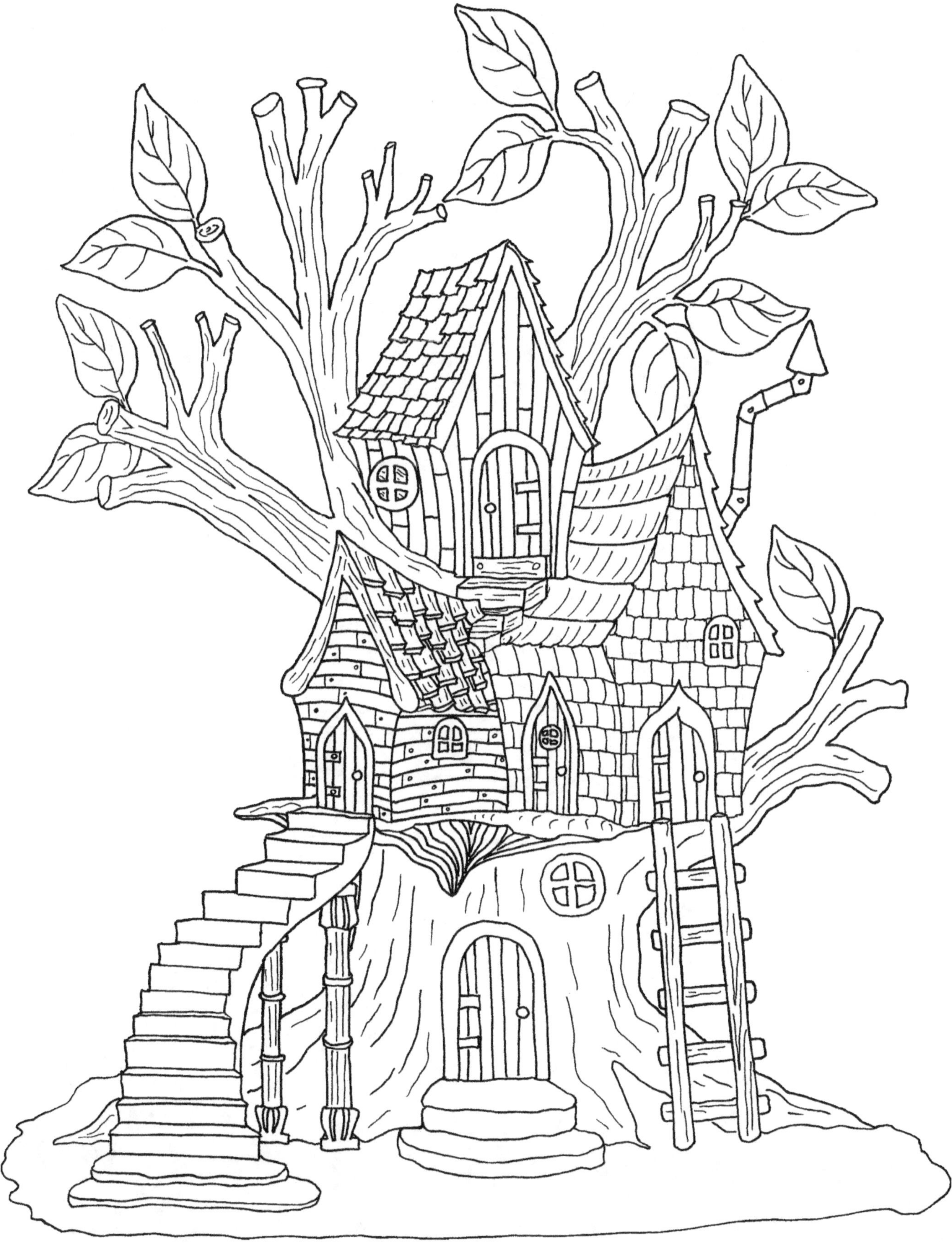

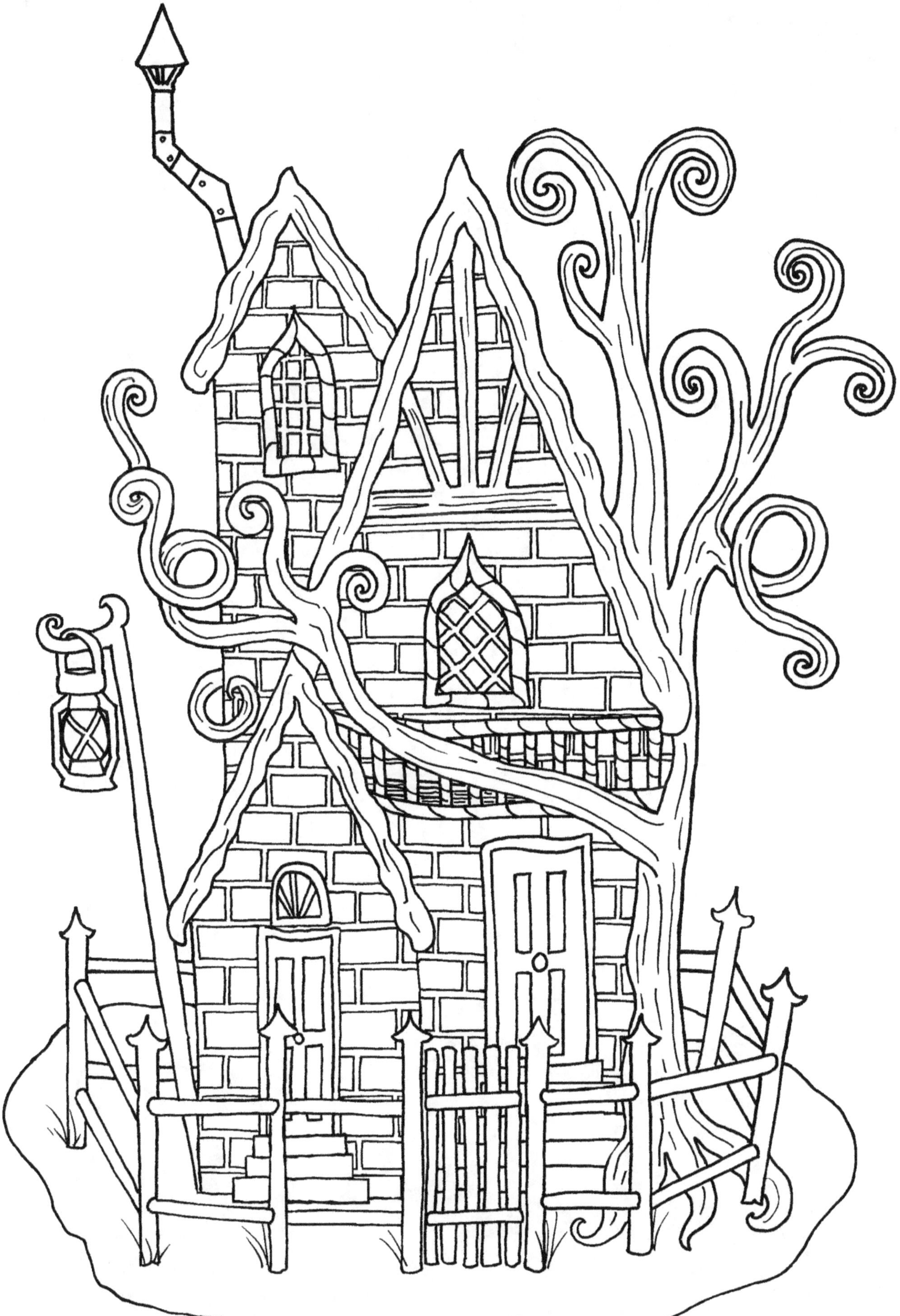

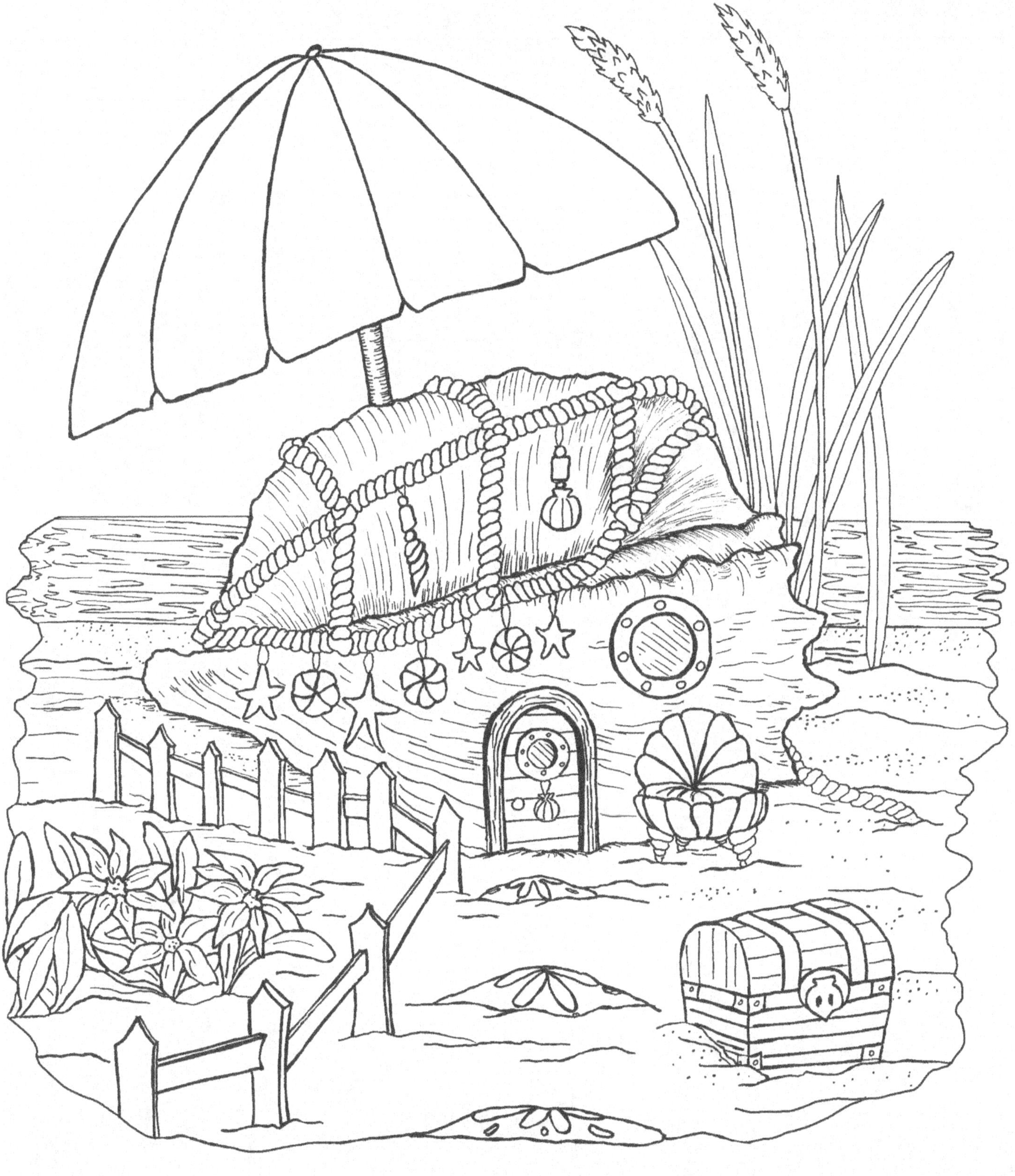

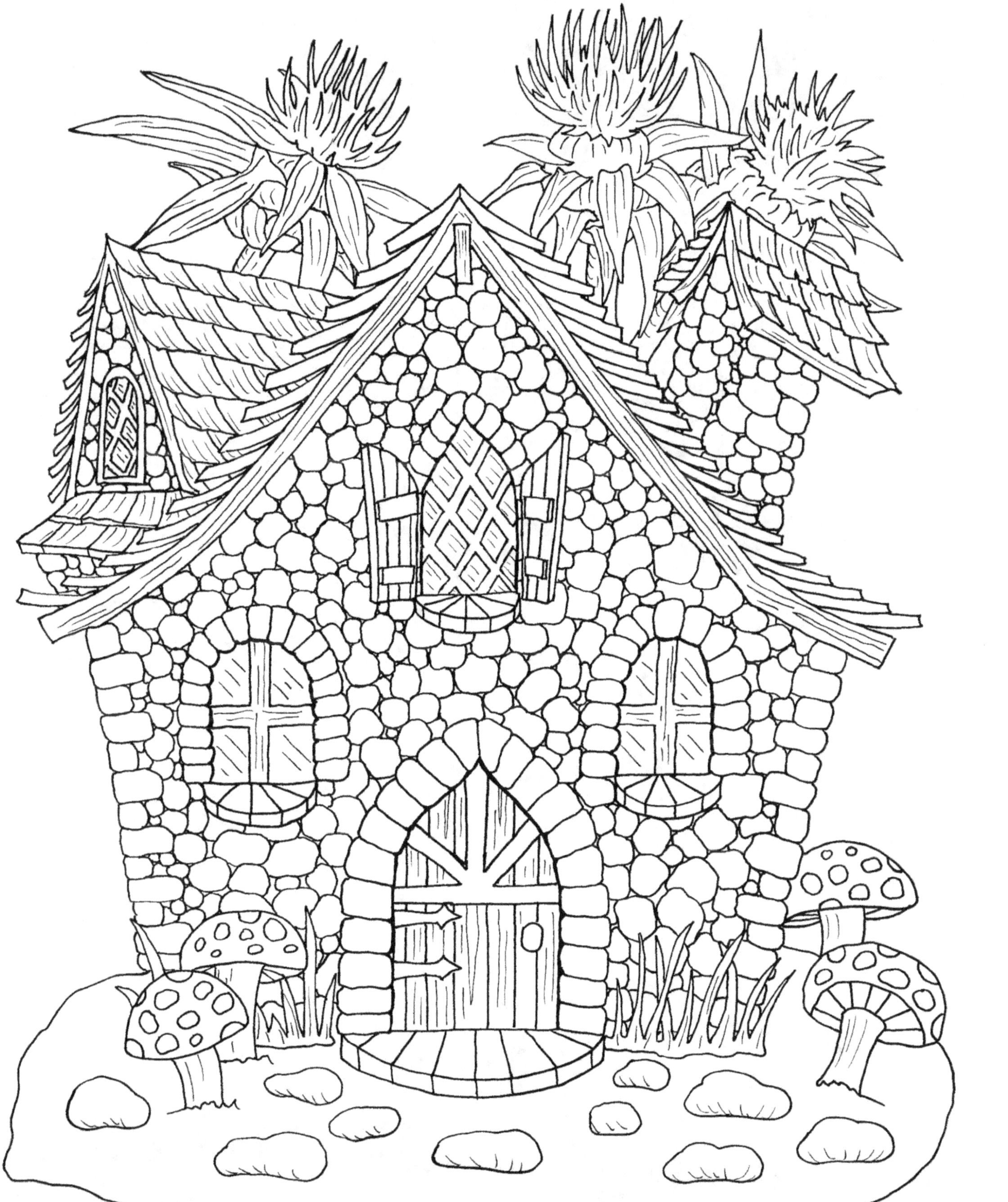

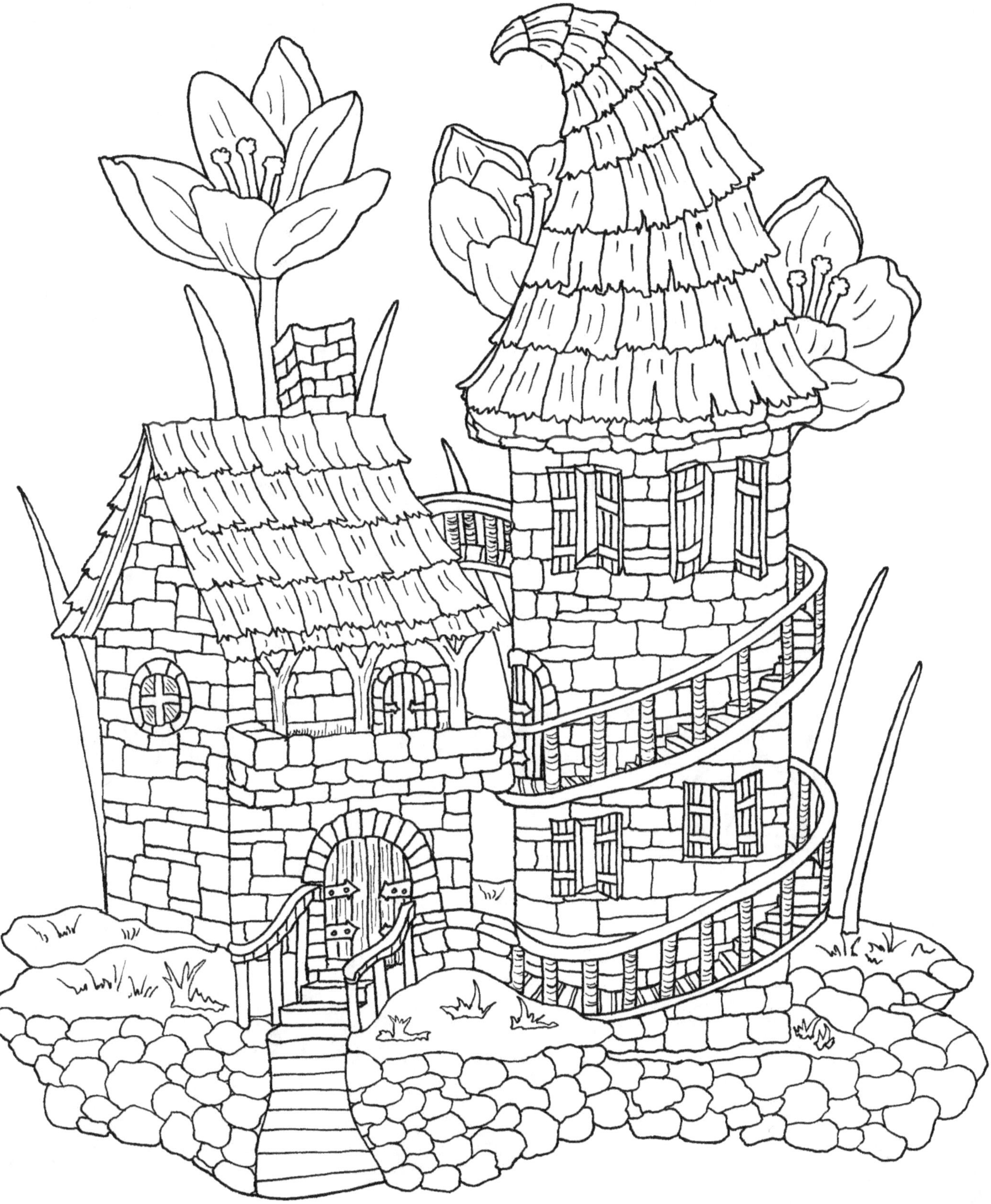

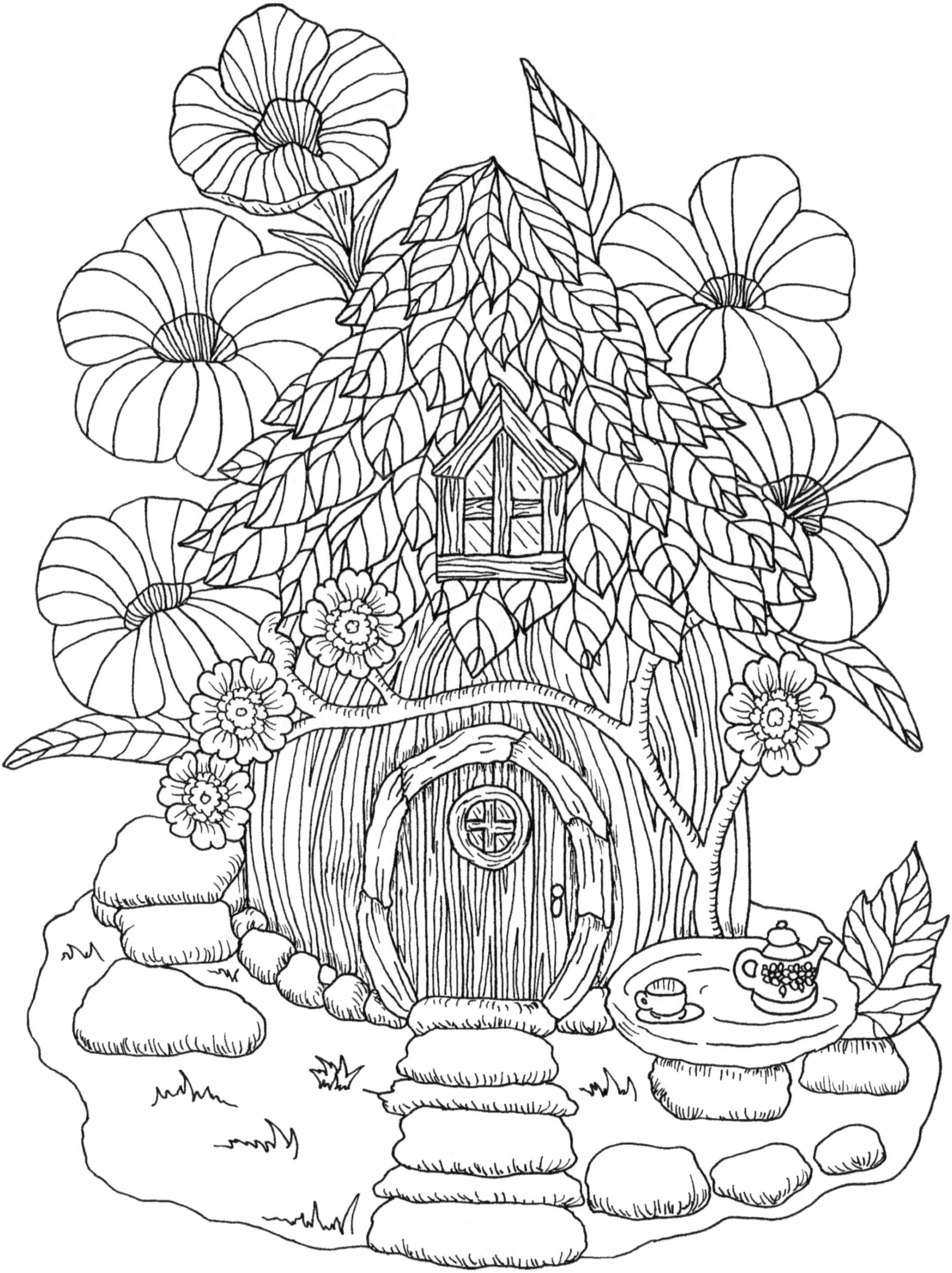

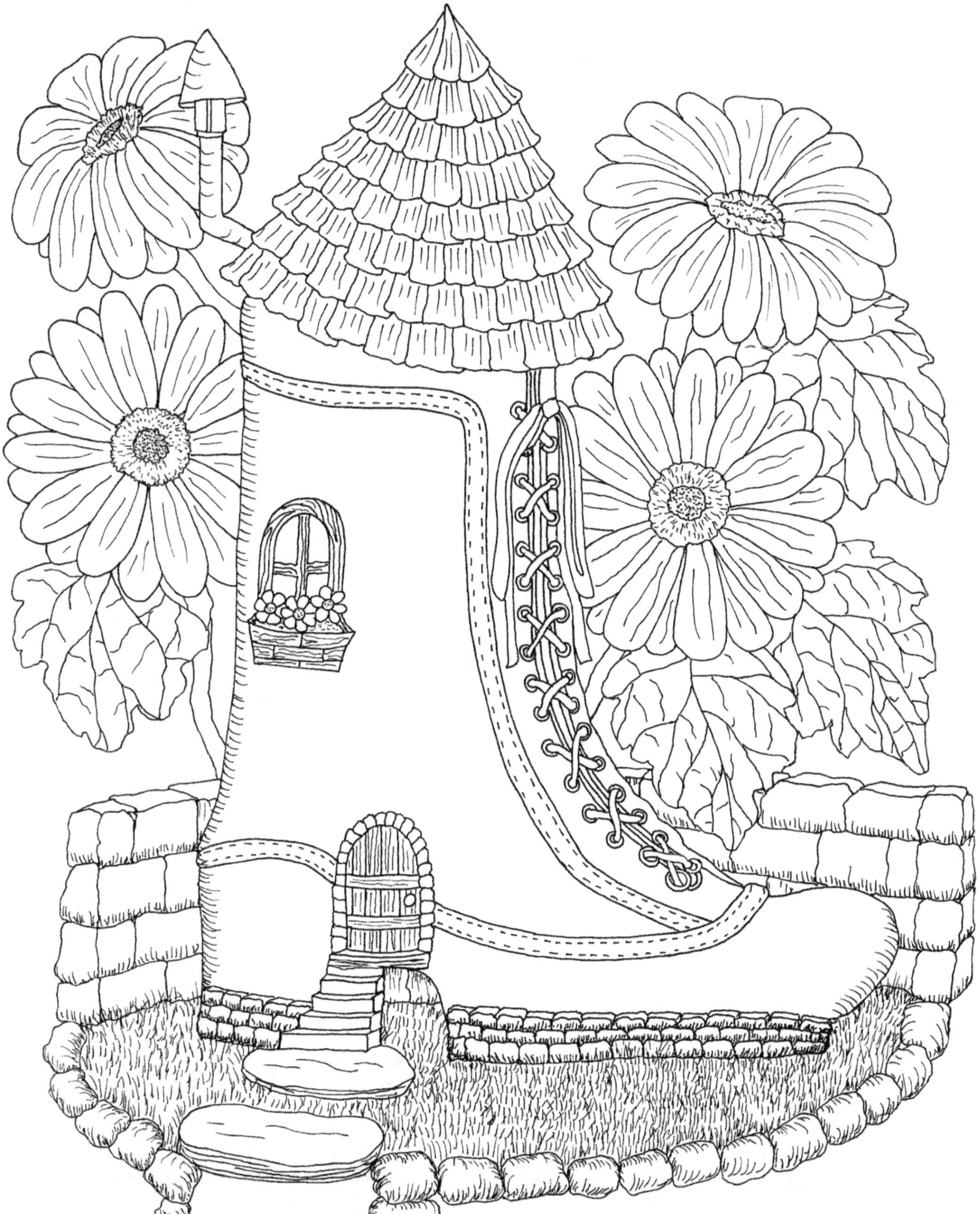

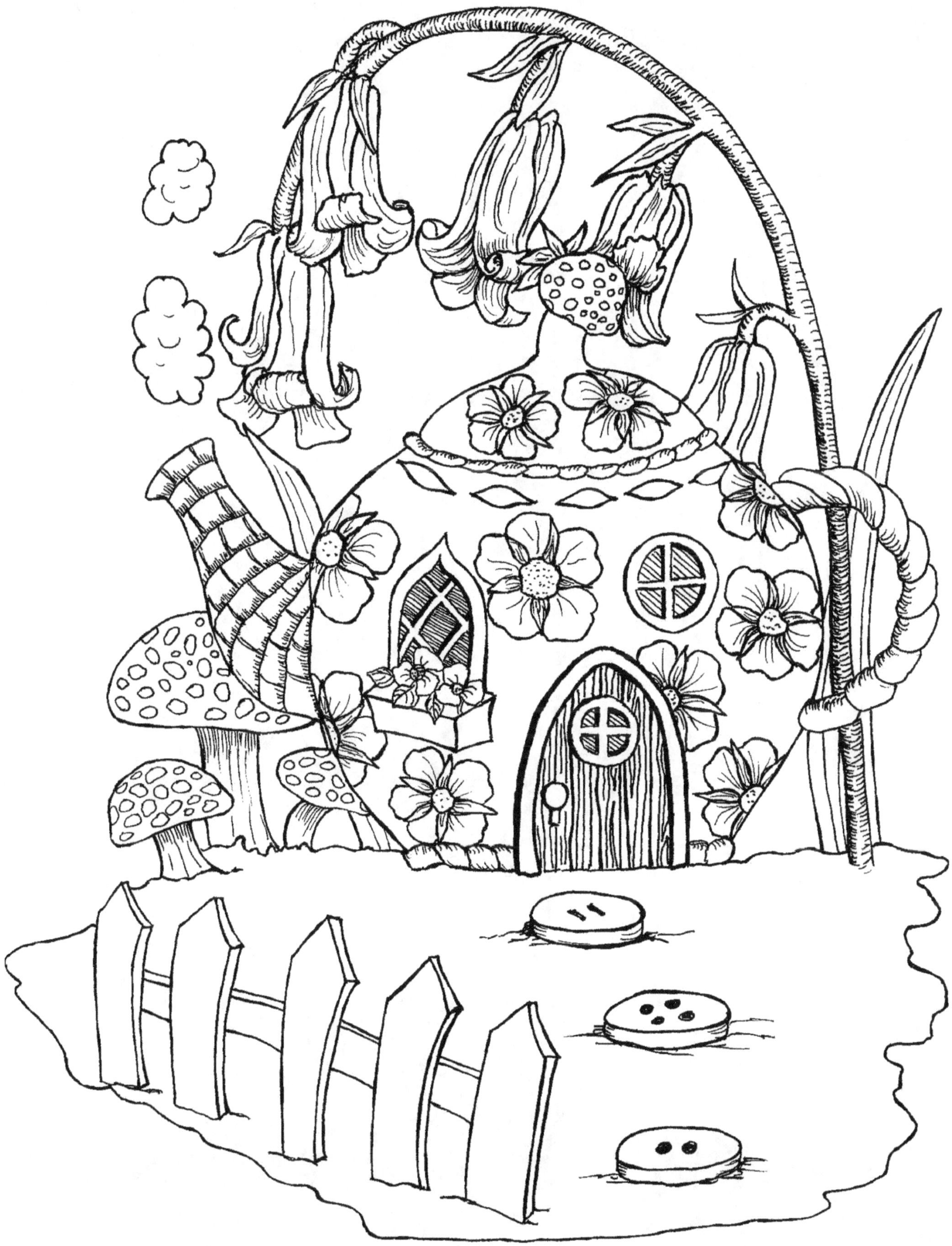

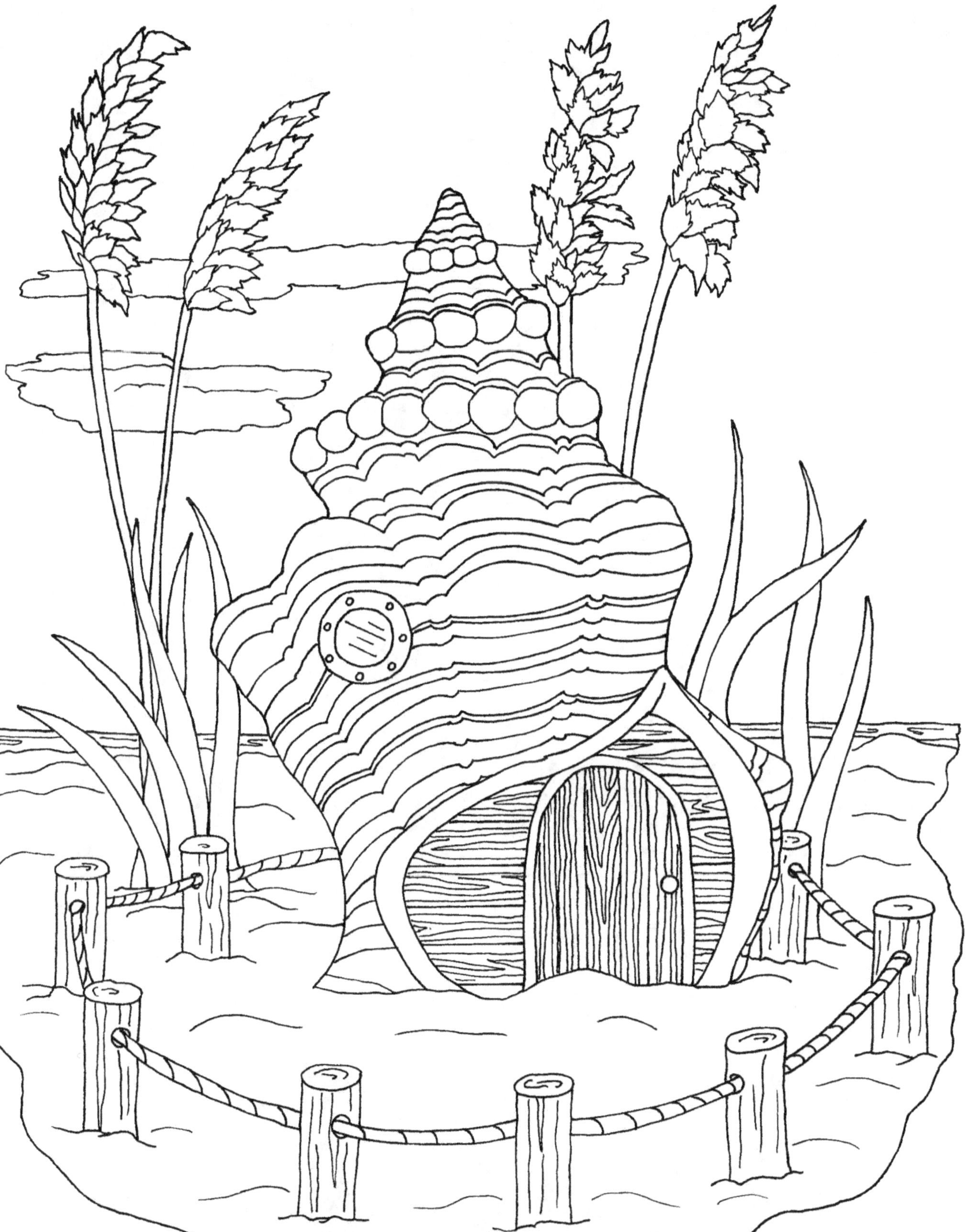

www.ingramcontent.com/pod-product-compliance
Lightning Source LLC
Chambersburg PA
CBHW080846170526
45158CB00009B/2648